BATON TWIRLING
is for me

BATON TWIRLING
is for me

Jim W. Hawkins

**photographs by
William Bible**

 Lerner Publications Company   Minneapolis

The author wishes to thank Tricia Hollingsworth and all the southern California twirlers who appeared in this book; their teachers; and the spiritleaders of San Diego, Madison, and Marian high schools for their encouragement. He also thanks his family, Tammy Clifford, and all others who made this book possible.

Photographs on page 7 by Linda K. Vittor. Photographs on page 8 courtesy of the Pal Twirlers, taught by Kathy Millett of the DMA.

To my family, and to all those who helped build the pastimes of twirling and cheerleading into true sports

LIBRARY OF CONGRESS CATALOGING IN PUBLICATION DATA

Hawkins, Jim W.
  Baton twirling is for me.

  (A Sports for me book)
  Summary: After learning and practicing the tosses, twirls, catches, tricks, and special routines of baton twirling, a girl enters a competition at the city fair.
  1. Baton twirling. [1. Baton twirling]
I. Bible, William, ill. II. Title. III. Series.
MT733.6.H38   791   82-245
ISBN 0-8225-1134-7   AACR2

Manufactured in the United States of America

International Standard Book Number: 0-8225-1134-7
Library of Congress Catalog Card Number: 82-245

2 3 4 5 6 7 8 9 10 91 90 89 88 87 86 85 84 83

Hi! I'm Tricia. I'd like to tell you about my favorite sport, baton twirling. I first became interested in baton twirling when I saw a twirler perform in a talent show on television. She could do amazing things with her baton, like tossing it high in the air and catching it behind her back. I decided I wanted to learn how to twirl, too.

My parents helped me find a good twirling teacher. Her name was Ms. Clifford. She said that she had been shy like me when she first started twirling. But performing had helped her overcome her shyness. Sometimes another teacher, Ms. Carr, helped me, too.

My teachers told me that baton twirlers can compete in three areas: **parade**, **corps** (KOR), or **solo performance**.

At the next parade I went to, I especially watched for the baton twirlers. They performed in front of the marching bands. Parade twirlers are also called **majorettes**.

I didn't want to spend so much time with a band, so I thought about twirling with a corps. A corps is a group that performs together in shows and contests. I watched a group called the Pal Twirlers. They moved together so perfectly! I knew that before I could develop that kind of teamwork, I'd have to be able to twirl well by myself. So I decided to start with solo twirling.

I practice twirling at least one hour every day. The first thing I do at every workout is warm up. I do arm circles, body twists, and leg stretches. I also jog to build my endurance. Baton twirlers need endurance because they can't take breaks during a twirling routine.

After I warm up, I work on my baton skills. Ms. Carr helped me select a baton that was the right length for me. Your baton should be about two inches longer than your arm. You grip the baton on the metal **shaft.** The smaller end is called the **tip,** and the fuller end is the **ball.**

Ms. Carr also showed me how to take care of my baton. I carefully wipe the baton before each practice. This helps me grip it more firmly. You should never put rosin or other waxes on the baton. If they dripped while being applied, they could harm the contest floor.

You must also check the baton for wear. When the tip is getting worn, you can sometimes see the shaft coming through. The old tip will have to be pulled off and replaced.

The more you drop the baton, the faster the ball and tip will wear out. And believe me, you'll drop your baton a lot! It takes a lot of practice to master even basic twirls, circles, and spins.

The first twirls I learned were the **horizontal twirl** and the **wrist twirl**. To do the horizontal twirl, grip the baton in the middle of the shaft. Your thumb should be pointing toward the ball. Extend your twirling arm out to the side. Your wrist will do the twirling. The ball should circle on top of your arm while the tip circles below.

The wrist twirl is similar to the horizontal twirl except that your twirling arm is held down at your side. A loose, relaxed wrist motion should move the ball forward and down so that the ball circles inside your arm. The tip will circle outside your arm.

There's a lot more to twirling than just moving the baton correctly. I also have to remember to control my whole body. Sometimes Ms. Clifford had to remind me to stand up straight with my stomach in and my shoulders back. It's easy to develop bad habits if you're not careful.

When you are twirling, the entire body must look graceful. The hand that isn't being used shouldn't be dangling or grabbing for the baton. It should be held on your waist or extended gracefully with closed fingers.

It is usually easiest to learn a twirl with your right hand first if you are right handed. If you are left handed, it's best to learn with your left hand first. You may have to work longer and harder to master the same twirl with your weaker hand.

Good twirlers, however, soon develop **ambidexterity**. Ambidexterity is the ability to use both hands equally well. With lots of practice, you can develop ambidexterity, too. Since my arms got tired easily at first, I was glad I could switch hands.

Another movement is the **circle**. Grip the baton in the center of the shaft with your thumb toward the ball.

While holding the baton out to the side, drop the ball down and away from your body making a vertical circle. The ball passes around your elbow. To add variety, you can move your twirling arm across your body or over your head while the circles are being made. Changing your arm positions make this move look more difficult.

Many beginning movements use only one hand. But the **two-hand spin**, as its name suggests, uses both hands.

For this move, the baton is held palm down in the right hand, thumb to ball. The right hand turns the baton clockwise. The left hand crosses under the right and grasps the ball end of the shaft.

Hook the thumb of your left hand around the shaft. The right hand then releases the baton, and both hands are moved apart.

The two-hand spin continues as you turn the baton over again. Now bring your first hand beside the baton, grip the shaft, and remove the other hand to complete the spin.

To add variety to this move, you can spin the baton around your waist or knees.

I learned the twirls, circles, and spin from a standing position, and now I was eager to twirl to music. Almost all competition baton routines are done to marching music. The marching step is called **strutting**. It takes practice to strut in perfect time with the music.

Always start marching with your left foot first. Bring your knee high, but keep your toes pointed down. Meanwhile, your right leg should be locked in a straight position. When you bring your left foot down, touch the ground toe first.

Next I learned more advanced baton skills like **passes, tosses,** and **rolls.** A pass is an exchange of the baton from one hand to the other. I learned the **thumb pass,** which requires a strong flick of the thumb to succeed. For this pass hold your thumb to the ball. The baton spins around the thumb and then it is exchanged to the other hand.

During a toss, the baton is thrown in the air. Twirls that are thrown high over the twirler's head are also called **aerials.** Your hands can go gracefully into many positions while the baton is in the air. They can be outstretched, held together, or held in other positions. When you can do aerials well, you can spin your body while waiting for the baton to come down.

Another way to vary tosses is to vary your catches, or **receptions**. The most simple reception is in front of the body because you can follow the baton with your eyes. *Always* keep your eyes on the *center* of the shaft while the baton is in the air. Try to catch it when it's just above your head. Grasp the shaft palm down, and then pull it down in front of your body.

The **blind catch** is much more difficult. This reception is made behind your back. Because you lose sight of the shaft for a split second before you catch it, you have to get the timing down carefully.

Twirlers do other receptions, like the one made while standing on one leg. The baton can be caught and tossed into another aerial or circled under the leg.

During a roll, the baton leaves your hands momentarily. But it remains in contact with other parts of your body before being controlled by the hand again. During an elbow roll, for example, the baton leaves your hand, travels around the arm and elbow, and is grasped once again by the hand.

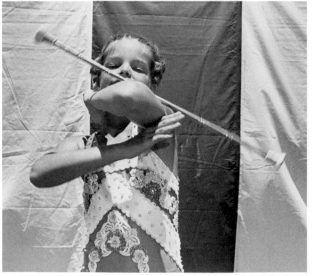

In a **body wrap**, the baton rolls around the neck, waist, and legs. This is a very difficult trick, but the challenge makes it fun.

The wrap usually begins with the baton in the left hand, thumb toward tip. Keep the baton horizontal as it rolls around the body. The baton is usually recovered with the opposite hand.

Ms. Clifford helped me put my baton skills to music. She taught me dance and gymnastics moves to add grace and smoothness to my routine.

One such move is the **lunge**. To do the lunge, bend one leg and point the toes on the other foot. You can hold the baton over your head, or you can twirl it.

Jumps and leaps are other ways to add graceful body movements to a routine. The jumps are similar to cheerleading jumps. The **split jump**, for example, is done like forward splits.

During the **spread eagle jump**, your body is held sideways. To do the **straddle jump**, face forward, bend at the waist, and hold your legs apart.

During each of these jumps, you can pass the baton between your legs while you are in the air. To prevent injury, take care to land on the balls of your feet.

As my baton twirling skills got better, I was eager to compete. The day finally came when Ms. Carr said, "Tricia, why don't you enter the competition at the city fair?" I was so happy that she thought I was ready for competition!

Ms. Carr explained how the contest would be run. The twirlers compete against others in their own age group and skill level.

The age groups usually cover a two- to five-year span. The contest in my area had age groups for twirlers 6 and under, 7 to 9, 10 to 12, 13 to 15, and for 16 and over. I would be competing in the 10- to 12-year-old group.

Your skill level is determined by the number of first-place awards you have won. I will be a beginner until I have taken first place in 8 competitions. Then I will compete at the intermediate level until I have taken 12 firsts. The advanced level is for winners of more than 12 contests.

The contestants perform in front of judges who will award up to 20 points in five areas: difficulty, baton speed, smoothness, variety, and showmanship.

Part of showmanship is having a nice smile, good eye contact, and a neat appearance. Your costume should be appropriate for your age group. You also need clean white tennis shoes and white socks.

I wanted to enter two events, so my mom helped me design two costumes. One was a leotard decorated with trim and glittering sequins. The other was a special costume for the **dance twirl** event.

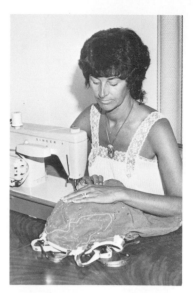

Dance twirl is a routine combining dance and baton twirling. As you twirl, you act out the story told by the music. The twirlers dress in special costumes. Some of the contestants were cowgirls and gypsies. I was a Spanish dancer, and I did my routine to Caribbean music.

I didn't get an award in the dance event, but just as I was starting to feel disappointed, another twirler said I had done really well for my first time out. It was nice to meet a friend who cared about me. Twirlers make lots of new friends at competitions.

Twirlers have developed two customs that show friendship and good sportsmanship. One custom is exchanging "good lucks." These are small gifts like food or fuzzy animals. They are nice reminders of past competitions.

The other custom is the traditional finger lock. You interlock the little fingers of your right hands in a quick shake.

As I waited for my next event, I watched other twirlers practicing. Some twirlers were studying the path of the sun so that they would be able to follow the baton in flight without getting blinded. Dropping the baton worried me a lot, but I knew that even national champions have drops. Drops are penalized by lowering your score half a point, but you just have to keep going.

Now it was time for my second event. I had to perform within a **lane**, a special area marked on the floor in front of the judges' table. I stood **at ease** with my feet apart and my baton held behind my back.

To begin, I stood **at attention** with my feet together and my hands on my hips. The baton was cradled in my right hand with the ball pointing toward the floor.

All solo routines start and end with a **salute**. This signal is important because it starts the clock that times your performance. All routines are timed, and you are penalized if your routine is too long or too short. To salute, bring your right arm across your chest to the left shoulder. The baton should be held vertically in your right hand with the ball pointing up.

After my event was over, the judges announced the awards. Although I did not win first place, I did win several other awards. Later everyone received their score sheets from the judges. They had many helpful comments for improving my performance.

After reading these comments, I stopped worrying so much about making mistakes. I spent more time practicing with my teachers and other students. We encouraged each other all the time.

One of my friends is a twirler named Damon. He wishes more boys would find out how strenuous and competitive baton twirling can be. Boys have their own style of twirling and compete in a special boys' division.

I continued working on my basic skills, but I also started to practice more advanced novelty twirling projects like the **Samoan knives, hoop baton,** and **fire baton.** I like Samoan knives best. They are two knives locked together at the tip by hooks. It is a real challenge to twirl them fast enough to keep them stable.

I wish I could compete with the knives more, but this event isn't offered at every competition. So sometimes I compete in the hoop event. The hoop baton has a fringed circle around it. I think the hoop baton looks pretty when you twirl it.

You must take special precautions before using the **fire baton**. You have to spray your hair and costume with flame retardant, and you have to have a special case handy to put out the fire. Only the padded ends of the baton are lit. The flaming baton looks very pretty at night.

As you advance, you can plan two-baton programs, or you can work with a friend. You can see that the sport of baton twirling is very challenging. I hope you'll try it and discover how fun twirling can be. I wish you the best of luck!

BATON TWIRLING Words

BATON SPEED: The rate at which the baton moves during a routine

BREAK: A point in a routine when the baton stops spinning

CENTER BALANCE: The point on the shaft where the weight of the two ends is even

CONNECTIONS: Simple moves to make a routine flow smoothly from one trick to another

DEAD STICK DROP: A strutting trick in which the baton is released and falls without spinning or rising

DROP: A loss of control resulting in the baton falling to the ground

FINGER TWIRL: Movement of the baton around the fingers

FLIP: A small, quick toss from one hand to the other

HORIZONTALS: A series of tricks, also known as *flats*, in which the baton stays level with the ground

LEAP: A jump off one foot onto the other. While in the air, the legs are split as much as possible.

LOFT: The rising action of a baton before it falls in a dead stick drop

LUNGE: A pose with the body weighted on one foot and the other foot pointed behind

PATTERN: The angle at which the baton spins

PENALTY: A reduction in your score: 1/2 point for a drop, loft, or out-of-step; 1/10 point for breaks, slips, off-patterns, and for each second of overtime or undertime

RECEPTION: The method of catching the baton

RELEASE: A toss of the baton

ROLLS: A series of moves making the baton travel around the elbows, arms, neck and legs

SHAFT: The metal part of the baton

SLIP: A mishandling of the baton that does not result in a drop

UNISON: More than one twirler doing the same tricks at the same time

VERTICALS: A series of tricks in which the baton stays at an up-and-down angle

WHIPS: Tricks done while holding the baton at one end and swinging it rapidly

ABOUT THE AUTHOR

JIM W. HAWKINS is active in the Baton Boosters Association of San Diego County, California. He is also a member of the National Baton Twirling Association and is chairman of the Committee for More School Spirit. A certified teacher, Mr. Hawkins coaches the San Diego High School cheerleaders. He also works with other youth sports and does freelance writing.

ABOUT THE PHOTOGRAPHER

WILLIAM L. BIBLE, JR., received his master's degree in industrial arts from San Diego State University. He has been an army photographer and a bullfight publicity photographer and has taught high school graphic arts and photography. Mr. Bible is currently a photography instructor in the San Diego area. His photographs have appeared in numerous magazines and newspapers.